REROUTED
The Way I Couldn't See

ERIC RAINEY

Rerouted: The Way I Couldn't See

Copyright © 2018 Eric Rainey

All rights reserved. No part of this book may be reproduced or transmitted in any form or by any means, electronic or mechanical, including photocopying, recording, or by any information storage and retrieval system without the written permission of the author or publisher, except where permitted by law.

ISBN: 978-1-949176-08-7 (paperback)
ISBN: 978-1-949176-16-2 (e-book)

Library of Congress Control Number: 2018909223

Edited by: Tecia Sellers
Exterior cover design by: Jacquis Hale

Published by: KRL Publishing

This Book is Dedicated in the Memory

of

Tarntanisha Rainey and
Murphy Lee Jamerson III

TABLE OF CONTENTS

Forward i

Chapter One: Early Years 1

Chapter Two: Moving 6

Chapter Three: My Toughness Developed 12

Chapter Four: My Brother's Keeper 21

Chapter Five: The Street Life 30

Chapter Six: Love Lost to Begin Love 37

Chapter Seven: The Encounters With God 42

Chapter Eight: Married to That Life 47

Chapter Nine: Church 52

Chapter Ten: Tragedy to Hope 61

Conclusion 66

Acknowledgements 68

References 70

FORWARD

Something about this book captured your attention. Perhaps it was the words on the cover, the cover design, or the author himself. One thing is for certain – if you have been carrying feelings of being redirected and rerouted, you were no doubt guided to pick up this book. This book is you! As Eric Rainey shares his life's journey on how he was redirected from the country roads of Arkansas, to the city streets of Wisconsin, towards a greater and deeper purpose in life, allow his steps to reassure you that this new path you are on is no mistake. Let down your guards, be present in this moment as the Lord will parallel this narrative with your life, to ensure you that you are on the right road. As Eric Rainey states, *"Somewhere in your journey God has rerouted you in your life."* Through the guidance of the Holy Spirit, God places us back on the road to a fulfilled purpose and designed destiny.

I have had the distinct pleasure of watching a dream of authorship to become realized through this young man, whom I have been privileged to call brother. Eric Rainey's rerouting experiences reinforce the reader to think of where they are in life now and to not allow missed opportunities that the reader may have experienced be a hindrance of forward progression. So what if your previous plans, decisions or investments did not work. They could not work for a reason. Your plan may have been good; but God's plan will lead you to your purpose.

Rerouted challenges you to perform an investigation by looking into a spiritual mirror and asking yourself: Are you being led by the Spirit or by your own desires? Whether the latter is true, one thing is for certain: God will reroute you. The rerouting is necessary as it reminds me of a scripture that says, *"He (God) who started a good work in you will complete it."* (Philippians 1:6)

Do not worry about reaching your destination; you will get there if you open your mind to receive the new route God is making for you. After all, Jesus was God's plan B. Jesus was a detour from the original plan. The Bible says what the first Adam could not do, God sent the second Adam (Jesus) to make it happen.

God can and will reroute you to get you to your destination.

Kimberly R. Lock
Author, Speaker, Publisher

REROUTED
The Way I Couldn't See

EARLY YEARS

Growing up was challenging, and quite entertaining. I was conceived in a small country town in Arkansas called Fordyce, and born in Milwaukee, Wisconsin on September 29, 1970. I remember being a little boy in Fordyce watching my grandmother boil water, so I could take a bath in this big silver tub. I am talking about a tub you can pick up and move to any room in the house. My grandparents did not have a bathroom or a toilet in the house at that time. There is nothing like being a scared little boy going outside in pitch black, with no street lights just to use the toilet. Are you kidding me, an outhouse? That was country life to the fullest.

It seemed like my grandmother would only go to the store to get tea and pop, that's what we called soda. It was a blessing to be able to go outside and pick whatever watermelon I wanted, or to see hogs, chickens, goats, and all types of vegetables that we ate. I didn't know it back then, but God had given me everything I needed. He was showing me at an early age that he was and is always in control. No running hot water, no problem we just heated water on the stove. One thing that did was ensure each person took a good bath and got up out the tub before the water got cold.

This place was special, even the air just smelled different. My family would all drive from different cities in the united states to come to Fordyce for the family reunion. Whoever came to Fordyce back then all stopped at my grandparents' house first, because coming into town it would be the first house of many houses that a family member would run into. After stopping at my grandparents' house, everyone proceeded to my great grandma Lace's house. Grandma Lace was the glue to the family and she was always strapped. Yes, she carried a pistol in her purse at all times, she was old school. This is the place everyone would get together for the family reunion and the entire family would be having a ball. Kids having dance contests, fireworks all over the place, food galore, and the older people just relaxing watching the kids having a ball. Half of Fordyce has to be related to me, from the Raineys, Mitchells, Marks, Cranfords, Edwards, and Taylors, all these families are related and all live in this little country town. God surrounded me with love, family, and the lasting memories of where I came from.

REROUTED

My grandmother knew something about me, but she would just say you are special. She protected me like she was a lion and I was her cub. In some ways I think my aunts and uncles thought I was spoiled, but she knew I had a calling on my life. I remember she would make me sleep next to her and she would say everything is going to be alright. I often wondered why my grandmother would always say that because to me everything was alright. They call that a mother's intuition, and she was right. You see God does the same thing, he comforts and protects. In Proverbs 30:5, it talks about His Word being pure, but also being a shield unto them that put their trust in Him. I never felt afraid as long as my grandmother was there, and to have to leave without her was devastating for me as a kid. I believe everyone has that person who can make you feel like you are the only person in the room, and the room has a thousand people in it. That's how I felt every time she looked at me.

Now my grandfather, he was different but laid back. He was known as Big Horn, because when he drove through town he would blow that semi horn long and loud. I loved to see him dip snuff, put his cap on, and be ready to roll. I got curious one day and tired that snuff for myself, never did I make that mistake again. Didn't know you couldn't swallow that stuff, I got sick and that was the end of my tobacco(snuff) chewing days, done! He was a very simple man who wanted the family to succeed. When I say simple that's exactly what I mean, he would wear nothing but overalls and a t-shirt. I laugh every time I think about him, because no matter how much money you gave him for clothes, he was going to buy some overalls!

Just watching my grandfather drive that semi-truck full of wood through town was like watching superman flying through the sky to rescue people. I guess that's why I love to drive trucks, buses, tractors, anything that is big. While sitting there on my grandparents' porch, Greyhound buses could be seen rolling through on their daily schedules, and I would often wonder what it would be like to get on the bus and get out of town. Well not only did we end up getting on the Greyhound to leave Fordyce, I ended up driving for them as well. I never thought in my wildest dreams I would ever drive for them, and I even had a desire to drive a Greyhound through Fordyce. Although that never happened, I still got a chance to live out one of my childhood dreams. To me, a person was going somewhere when he got on that bus, getting away from his past and letting that "dog" take him to his future.

Everything that happened back then has directly impacted and shaped my life to some degree. I have learned that, you will always be exposed to something you may do in your life at an early age. Your beginnings will talk to you when you become an adult, to let you know that thing you wanted as a child, you can have it. That childlike faith, believing you would do those things you desired as a child, is the same faith you must have today. I tell my children all the time that I had it made

REROUTED

back then, everything I buy now I had right in my own backyard. As I reflect, I never thought I'd miss a place so much. I didn't realize until I became an adult, the peace, the beauty, and the serenity that came along with that place. Although it was a slow paced, southern, country place, it's what I needed. A lot of people call me country to this day, they say I'm real laid-back and easy going. That's just in me, that's where my roots are from and I can't get away from that.

Nowadays, the same problems that we have in the city of Milwaukee, we have those same problems in the small country town of Fordyce – people on drugs and stealing – same issues just a smaller place. The difference is everybody knows everybody so you're probably not going to get away with a lot of things in the country as you would in the city. I would have never thought as a child that Fordyce would have some of the same problems as the big city. People think living in the country is just farming and tobacco chewing, but that narrative change quickly. Drugs have a way of finding a place where it's wanted. God's timing is impeccable and He rerouted my life just in time, He wanted me to see the things when I needed to see them and return when needed.

MOVING

I recall moving back to Milwaukee, WI when I was 5 years old. We moved to a place called Parklawn, which folks call the projects. Let me tell yawl something, having a bathroom with hot water by just turning the knob was priceless. Even the toilet was in the same room. No more going outside to *"handle my business,"* you know what I mean. I felt like the Jefferson's, you know, George and Wheezy. From the outhouse to the projects, this was a penthouse to me. I thank God for allowing me to see what can happen when you leave your nest, your comfort zone.

My mom decided that she didn't want us to grow up in the same place she did, she saw better and ran for it. My darling mother worked her fingers to the bone. She did everything she could to keep food on the table and clothes on our backs. This woman even took a job as an ice cream cart driver; well more like a motorized

REROUTED

bike. All the boys I played basketball with saw her one day selling ice cream and laughed me right off the basketball court. I was so embarrassed and hurt by the teasing and being made fun of. Nevertheless, my mom continued to drive the ice cream motor-bike so we could have better. Now that I am a grown man I understand she was just showing me that a person must work to get the things he or she wants in this world. She also taught me it doesn't matter what others think of you, if God is pleased with you, that's what matters. The work ethic that she displayed was key to the development of me and my brothers. I used to wonder how she was able to make it, I know now that it had to be by the grace of God. You mean to tell me in this cruel world that a single mom can raise her sons, cook, feed, bathe, wash and give them a whooping at the same time? They don't make them like this anymore. Did I mention my mom had a degree in "whoop ology?" Let's just say she never spared the rod. I tell you this woman was short and gifted, the power and force that she possessed could wake up the neighborhood. By the time she got done whooping your behind, you didn't do that no more. I tell her they would put her in jail today, she would laugh and say oh well you must be disciplined.

I thought she was wonder woman. She would get up early make me and my brother Damian breakfast and take us to the sitter Ms. Coleman. She would then proceed to walk to the bus stop to catch the bus to work. My mother always made sure we ate and took our baths before we went to bed. Whenever I got sick she would rub Vicks all over my body and tell me everything would be ok. There's nothing like a mother's love.

There is a song I still remember singing to my mom by the Manhattans called, "Shining Star." Some days I could tell when she was feeling down, I would grab the microphone and plug it into the jukebox we had and sing my little heart out. The smile on her face every time I would sing that song made me happy. I love my mother dearly, she never turned her back on me even when I was wrong, she encouraged me to do right. We didn't always have the best, but we had love. This is being rerouted to the uttermost, because when we moved to Milwaukee we had a transition that was scary for us.

I didn't mention the fact that we didn't have food some days and the manager at the Ambassador Hotel was really God sent to allow us to stay there with no money, this took place right before we moved to Parklawn. There used to be this Big Boy restaurant not too far from the hotel, I would walk over there with my bother Damian to watch people eat their food. I would tell De (Damian) I'm going to buy you some food one day from here. Imagine seeing people throw away most of their food and you are starving. Most of the people inside were white folk with their families having a great time. Have you ever been so close to something you needed and couldn't have it? That's how I felt. Just so

REROUTED

you know I eventually took De too Big Boys and we ate burgers with shakes not wasting a thing.

The anguish on my mom's face when there was nothing to eat was hurtful, and when we did get a little to eat she would take jelly and bread and cut it into small pieces, we thought we had a lot on those days. Jesus fed 5,000 people with five loaves of bread and two small fish after he gave thanks. As hard as it was at that time, he didn't let us starve to death. I am grateful he still took care of us, when it seemed we were all alone. Therefore, I cherish our days in Parklawn, because that was our come up from not having much at all. Parklawn also was the place where I lost my best friend Sam who was hit by a car. I never saw Sam again after that, that hurt me. The penthouse got old quick, our house got broken into and things seemed to change by the minute. Ultimately, we moved back to Arkansas, this time to the city of Little Rock.

I used to wonder why we got to move all the time and everybody else seemed to stay where they always lived. I didn't know that the encounter that was about to happen would change my view of what family meant. This is where I met my cousin Murphy. I thought something was wrong with him the way he came and destroyed my train set the minute he got to our house. I told my mom he had to go, well I didn't know his mother had passed away and he was hurting. Come on, you know how they treat kids when hiding information, this is grown folks' business. From that very day we become brothers. I am asked just about every day if Murphy is my brother, well we look alike I just don't sign the checks. As a matter of fact, Murphy is one of my mentors. I can talk to him about anything and he will lead me to the Bible for all the answers to my issues. Having been a successful business owner of several daycares, he put in the work to get where he is today. Just to think how Murphy, Elvis (my brother), and I would run the streets and have a ball, but God has taken all 3 of us and put us in a ministry that we all serve in.

I often think about what if Murphy never came and stayed with us or we didn't move back to Arkansas at that time. So, I started thinking about Moses, what would have happened to him if Pharaoh's daughter never would have seen the ark in which he was in. God will make a way for his people to fulfill his purpose for you no matter the circumstance, I would have never saw as a child the man Murphy would become, only God can see that far. Murphy helped me reroute my mind set on a lot of issues that have helped me to become the man I am today. I am not perfect by any stretch of the imagination but having people around who are willing to push me to higher heights is critical.

I know Murphy just wants the best for me, so he goes out of his way to make sure I understand what this life is all about. I often think about when we get old and gray, we will buy some land and build some huge

REROUTED

houses in Fordyce and just sit back and think about how life was. It is so amazing to me that we made it this far considering how we used to be in the streets. I wish I can get a dollar for each time that somebody called me Murphy I'd probably be rich. I know God has some huge things in store for Murphy because he is a giver and he loves God. There is nothing that Murphy won't do for anybody, I've seen it from my own eyes. Some moves are necessary and some moves are ordained by God, and this move was necessary not only to help my mother at the time but also to help Murphy because he needed somebody at that time.

Oftentimes we don't get a chance to choose what we will do for others. Sometimes God chooses for you, to reroute your understanding about what God wants you to do. I truly believe we moved back just for that moment, because we were not there long. God is the ultimate chess player, he knows your next move, because he ordained it.

MY TOUGHNESS DEVELOPED

Well we moved back to Milwaukee and yes it was the projects, Westlawn! This place had a reputation for being real rough. I had some cousins who lived there and they didn't play no games. I recall going to play basketball and it seemed like everybody was much stronger than I was. My cousin Tank came and told me to, *"man up and play ball cuz."* I was elbowed, hit in the stomach, knocked down to the ground, it was brutal. Finally, I started to grow and everything that used to hurt me on the court, didn't anymore. I knew I belonged when I started to get picked by everyone to run with them. That just means playing with them.

In some ways that is exactly how life is, you start off timid in something and once you get that confidence in yourself you begin to take off. Once others see you

REROUTED

have confidence in yourself they are likely to pick you because of it. That was the way of life in Westlawn, either you played ball or you sold drugs. In the winter we would meet up at the Silver Spring Neighborhood Center to go indoors to play basketball. If you could play you were on the court all the time, we had people like Dwayne (Sweet hands) Mitchell, Scott Spinks, Freddie Riley, Jamal (Boo), Calvin Rayford and Terrance Ellis just to name a few ball players that could play with or against anybody. We would play all day, it kept us out of a lot of trouble. You know trouble has a way of finding you on the court, people calling bogus fouls or traveling knowing that wasn't the case. The arguments start and Brother Bob had enough, and it was lights out, everybody must leave.

Although it was Westlawn, and people were afraid to come to Westlawn without knowing somebody, it wasn't as bad from the inside as many would think. I loved the fact that we weren't robbing each other or breaking into our neighbors' house. We looked out for one another; even though there were drug dealers, pimps, hypes, and just straight up hustlers, they all got along. That was never more evident than when my mother got sick and was in the hospital for several weeks.

Our neighbor, Miss Francis, would fry chicken and pork chops for me and my brothers and I would make the sides. Yes, I would get in the kitchen and make up stuff and most of the days my brothers loved it. Now there were some days, well let's just say they wouldn't eat that again. I was growing up fast just trying to survive being a big brother with responsibilities at a young age. I have to give my brothers credit they didn't cause me any problems. I knew they depended on me, but I also depended on them.

Being lonely without my mom was hard somedays, just my brothers laughing or playing around put me at ease. I couldn't understand why I had to be the one carrying all this weight on my shoulders, but God knew I could do what I thought I couldn't do. No longer was I the teenager just hanging out with my friends, I was rerouted to be the man of the house, to protect and make sure my brothers were ok while my mom was gone away. My mom finally got out of the hospital and I got buck wild. I was drifting looking for a different lifestyle, just something new to do.

I started playing chess. I even played on a chess team at Wilbur wright middle school. This game took my mind off the things I did not have and made me become tactical. I mean I was always thinking. I remember playing with this man named Ray. He would ask me to play and he was good. It took me sometimes to beat him, but once I did I could not lose to him. Grown men do not like losing to a teenager, let's just say the invitation to play came less and less to not asking at all.

My dad, Alvin Taylor, used to tell me all the time, son you really don't have friends. I used wonder why he

REROUTED

would say such a thing. Well when he was in his 20's he got into an altercation with a man at a tavern. The man ultimately shot my dad and my dad took the gun from this man and shot him. The people that were with my dad all ran and left him. I finally understood what he was saying. People will leave you when things get rough, but I know God will never leave you nor forsake you, according to Heb. 13:5. I must give my dad credit, he took me as his own.

Ok I know you are wondering what's going on here. Well let me explain. Al is not my biological dad, but you could never tell when I was a little boy. I always wanted to be just like him. Pops was always cool like he was that dude. Whenever I needed anything he was right there. He always told me and my brother to try golf and tennis. He had visions of us playing golf in the early 80's. Pops did not play no games though he would protect us at any cost. My dad would come by sometimes and talk with my mom and somedays they would fight. My dad would not back down from anyone, he did not care who it was or where they came from. He could care less. My dad realized that getting into it with my mom was making me and my brothers upset, he soon stopped, and they would never fight again. Going over to pops' house on the weekends was cool, I got to see my sister Linda, my pops' wife Jamie, and my older brother Elvis when he would come for the summer. Elvis lived in Kingsland, Arkansas and we always anticipated his arrival every summer. It seemed like he got taller every time he came back. Elvis is 6'6"

ERIC RAINEY

now, I'm 5'10" and I was the one eating folks up on the basketball court go figure.

In 1988 somebody came to me and said Al is not your daddy. I thought they were playing a joke on me, but I looked at their face and it was a serious look. I walked around reflecting to when I used to say to myself my brothers don't look like me. I'm dark skinned and they were not dark at all. I remember over hearing people talking about Jesus and all that he can do for you. I saw a man on a western movie praying and he was on his knees, so I prayed and asked Jesus to be my dad. I was hurting bad. I asked my mother to tell me the truth and she did, she said Al is not your biological father.

I called my grandmother, she said she could hear the hurt in my voice and I could hear the hurt in hers as well. My grandmother arranged for me to meet the man who they said was my dad. I went to my grandparents' house in Fordyce, Arkansas and a man in a brown pick-up truck pulled up and introduced himself as Willie Clyde Edwards. I remember telling him my name but the whole ordeal was just awkward to me. He wanted me to meet his family, so we drove around going to different homes throughout Fordyce being introduced to the family. Everyone was overjoyed and happy except me, the only thing I could think of was AL. I was wondering why he never told me, I started to think he never had any intention. It was meant for me to meet Willie Clyde and get to know him, he was a kind man

REROUTED

who was just trying to feel me out at the time. It was cool, though I couldn't shake the bitterness I had toward everybody involved in this matter. This was a problem to me, why all the lies? If you knew you were my dad why didn't you come for me? Why tell me now AL is not my dad? Those were the questions going through my mind that I never asked.

Ultimately Willie Clyde and I had a good relationship. Howbeit, he passed away August 5th, 2011 of lung cancer. Willie Clyde had a daughter, Kim Edwards (my sister), who has spent most of her adult life in the Army serving our country. We didn't get a chance to spend a lot of time together, but I thank God for her. Hopefully we can sit down and have an intimate talk about life, what could've been and what can be in the future.

My mother was never married to AL or Willie Clyde, but God had a man waiting for her in a small town called Malvern, Arkansas. My mom got married to the love of her life, Mr. Jimmie Fondren Sr. This man showed my mom love she never experienced, a God-fearing man who loved God. I had never seen my mom smile the way she smiled when they were together. I still to this day can hear his voice when he called to tell me they went shoe shopping, AGAIN. He was so proud to sit there while she would try on shoe after shoe after shoe, a real man right there. In a strange way he was showing me what marriage should look and be like. I mean they went to church together, traveled everywhere together, they did everything together. He used to tell me all the time to have faith in God. I was like ok I hear you, but I am not on that right now. One day he sang a song called, *"Lord Thank You Sir,"* and it moved me to tears. This man could sing with the best of them, he was simply amazing. I know he was trying to steer me in the right direction, truth be told he was doing a great job. I began to sing that song I heard him sing, *"Lord Thank You Sir"* whenever I could, it seemed to relax me.

Mr. Jimmie and I had a great relationship, along with his son Jimmie (Skip) Fondren, Jr. and Beverly, Skip's wife. We gained a brother Skip in this union and 2 sisters, Jerri Fondren and Wyvonia Harris. Mr. Jimmie Hue Fondren, Sr. died January 25, 2007. Although Mr. Jimmie wasn't my dad, he left me with the memories of seeing my mother happy like never before.

I will always honor the fact that Willie Clyde is my father biologically, but AL will always be my dad no matter who says what. I have in me Al's swagger and his toughness. I became what I was exposed too. I believe God allowed this, so I can be bold in this season of my life. God wants what is best for his children, even if that child has his identity rerouted from birth. I understand now that God's plans for our lives are not always smooth. Even as a child he protects you by moving you into strategic places, though they may seem dark at times God knows exactly what he is doing.

REROUTED

I really didn't want to mention that chapter of my life. The shame, the feeling of what if, and the pain associated with this ordeal about who is and who isn't your dad was challenging. To see my mom get married to someone who loved her, then to see her feeling alone all over again after the death of her husband. John McDonnell once said, *"Each time we encounter a painful experience, we get to know ourselves a little better."* Although going through the process didn't feel good, I got through it. *"A bend in the road is not the end of the road unless you fail to make the turn,"* John Maxwell, The Law of Pain.

I found out I was way tougher than I ever imagined. I am not talking about physical toughness, I'm referring to the mental toughness I developed through this process. When that deep, deep pain comes up in your life it can consume you into thinking beyond your natural thoughts. It's like coming out of your comfort zone to confront something you can't hide from. Nothing is by chance when God is involved, if he placed the stars in the firmament, he surely knows how to place us where he wants us.

My pain pales in comparison to the pain his son Jesus endured for the betterment of our lives. When you are unlearned of that pain that Jesus went through you will always have a pity party for yourself. Jesus was the toughest of the toughest and that will never be matched. We equate tough to the streets and gangsters, when the truth of the matter is that tough is

ERIC RAINEY

a mindset that is developed by past pain. I developed thick skin through all of this and I learned the truth is not always told, but life has a way or showing up when we don't want it to. If I can tell any parent please tell your child who their father or mother is, don't have them wait for so long and don't hold on to a lie that could affect that child for the rest of his or her life. Although I do believe that this particular case was ordained by God, but all the cases are not so. When your pain turns into the development of your toughness it must put you on your knees first, and when it does you get up better off than you were before. Pick yourself up and let God lead the way.

MY BROTHER'S KEEPER

I was sleeping one night, and I had a terrible dream. I was sweating really badly, and my heart was racing. I dreamed somebody had shot my brother Damian and it scared me to the point I couldn't go back to sleep right away. Finally, I dozed off and my doorbell rings, so I go downstairs to answer the door and the police are standing there. They ask me do I know Eric Rainey, I'm like yeah you are talking to him. The police had the nerve to ask me was I sure, I said, *"Yes, I am Eric Rainey."* They began to say if you are Eric Rainey then who is the guy who got shot at Next Best Thing Night Club? I'm like officer I don't know who that could be, but it certainly isn't me. My mind starts to wonder about the dream I just had, I am convincing myself that it couldn't be Damian, the police would know that by getting his ID if that was the case and if De would have gotten shot one of his homies would have come by the house to tell me.

I remember I had to work the morning shift the next day which was a Saturday, and while I was working I received an emergency phone call stating, *"your brother has been shot in the head and he is undergoing emergency surgery right now."* I rushed to the hospital and when I arrived my mom and dad were already there along with my aunts and friends. I was thinking somebody had to have known last night that De got shot, because my mom lived in Arkansas at the time and she beat me to the hospital. I could see the pain and hurt on my family members' faces. When De came out of surgery they rolled him into the room and I couldn't even see his face. They had him wrapped up like a mummy. I was so angry, I just wanted to know what happened.

Wolf, one of my brother's homies, was there when everything went down. He began to tell me that our childhood friend Brian also got shot and the girl that Brian was dancing with at the time was killed by a bullet aimed at him. I asked Wolf what happen, he says a guy that they had been beefing with knew the security guard and dude let this man in with a gun. No one else had a gun in the place, because they were checking for such. My brother didn't stand a chance since the playing field was not even, he couldn't bring his protection in to ward off his attacker.

Now I am on a mission to find out who this person is that shot my brother and was trying to get at him, I

REROUTED

was ready to seek and destroy. I already knew I didn't have to be close to this individual to touch him, I come from a family of hunters and I was in the military as well. From my perspective, I was imagining putting a hole in this person's body big enough to see through. I didn't need anybody else to help me, I was ready. I went outside in the front of my house, and there was this detective sitting there watching me. He decided to get out of his police car and began to talk to me like he knew what my plans were. I'm thinking, I haven't told anybody what is about to go down and this man is saying things like revenge is not the answer, we will get the attacker. I just looked at the detective and said, *"we shall see."*

I opened up to my dad and told him what I was thinking, and he said, *"ok, but we got to let the police handle this one."* I could tell he was trying to protect me, but what he didn't know was that I felt like I was going to protect us all. I'm thinking, what if this dude come to the hospital and try to finish him off? My mind was not right, and I was looking for anybody who looked suspicious. I decided to stay at the hospital at night and sleep in the same room my brother was in, so did my dad. We weren't going to get caught slipping, so we were ready for anything. My mind kept telling me to listen to that detective and to my dad, but my heart was in a deep place. What that detective did was plant a seed that my dad confirmed by telling we gone let them handle their business. To my surprise, they end up finding the attacker and he was taken into custody.

ERIC RAINEY

They ended up finding this man guilty.

My life would have been destroyed if I never encountered that detective, he helped me to reroute my course of action. Just to think, I even wrote a track to it on a rap album I made shortly after this event. It wasn't pretty at all. You see, I was always reminded of what happened to my brother whenever I saw the scar on his head from his surgery, and there is no doubt in my mind that God changed the course of events that would have taken place. My brother is alive, and he is feeling pretty good, considering the fact he could've been dead. After all the fights we had growing up, I could only think about him being my little brother sitting in the back seat of my mom's Thunderbird eating all the sandwiches she made and falling asleep while my mom made me look at all the highway signs on the freeway and told me to remember them.

Funny how life works. About 7 months later I ended up going to the hospital because I was feeling terrible, something was seriously wrong. Come to find out after a series of tests the next day, the nurses were running me down the hall so I could have emergency surgery to save my life. I was told I had an abscess in my lower intestine that had burst and caused a hole in my intestine. They said, *"we have to do this surgery now or you could die."*

After a couple hours I was back in my room and there was De waiting for me along with my mom and my dad. If anyone knows my brother, he was thinking

REROUTED

somebody had something to do with this and it is on. So, he says, I am going to stay at your house to make sure everything is good. That is what makes him unique, he had just gotten shot 7 months ago and he was willing to protect me at all costs. I stayed in the hospital for 30 days. It was brutal, but De was the one who had to pick me up from the hospital and care for me the first week.

I lived upstairs in a duplex and the doctor wanted me not to be up and down stairs. I couldn't see it when we were little boys that we would have to take care of each other as adults. Truly we have been through a lot together, but what we went through made us stronger for the time we truly needed each other.

My youngest brother Kevin was living in Malvern, Arkansas when I got a phone call that he had been in a major car accident. I was saying to myself everything is going to be alright once they said he was alive, but they had to take him to the hospital. Well come to find out, everything was not okay. He had broken a bone in his leg and it was bad. The break was so bad that they had to leave the flesh open for a long period of time. Now you know if flesh is open like that it leaves a real bad smell. He called me himself from the hospital and he was crying because they told him they might have to cut his leg off. He asked would I pray for him and that his leg will be okay. Immediately, I told my wife and she told her grandparents who were the pastors of our church and they began to pray.

ERIC RAINEY

My wife and I decided to drive down there to be with him and to comfort him. When we walked in his room I could barely take the smell, but I couldn't show it because I knew he needed strength for me. They end up putting a rod in his leg, but that flesh still needed to be open for some time. My wife couldn't bear the smell, she was standing in the room for a little while and go out. I understood where she was coming from but there was no way I could leave no matter how bad the smell got. I felt that just being there made him feel a whole lot better and I think it helped his healing process.

Sometimes just being there in someone's presence can turn a whole situation around. I could see his confidence growing, he started feeling better about himself and next thing you know he was getting out the hospital. I thank God that he put it on our hearts to drive to Arkansas and to be in the hospital room with Kevin, because he needed that. There was nothing more that I could do besides pray and be there. There was nothing else I could think to do because there was nothing else to do. From that moment on I began to realize, not only was I his brother but I was like his spiritual advisor as well. Kevin didn't go to church, but I know he believed at that very moment when he asked us to pray for him. Today, Kevin is walking, and he still has his leg. He's doing pretty good for himself, although he can't stand for a long period of time he just thanks God that he has his leg. Every time I see Kevin, we call him big Cal, I think about that leg and what could have happened.

REROUTED

Now my brother Elvis he was the one that I tried to emulate as a child and in my early adulthood. My dad always called him Slim because he was tall and skinny at first. He is still tall, but he isn't real thin like he used to be. I recall being about 19 when Elvis used to ride through Westlawn in his Nissan 240xs coming to pick me up and going to hang out for a little while. We'd ride through the city of Milwaukee bumping Too Short, and I would be talking on his phone that came in the car. Man, I thought I was the stuff hanging with my big brother! Everybody in Westlawn thought he was a big-time dope dealer and that was not the case, he was working, and he had a lot of swag.

One night we were hanging out and we started drinking a whole lot, but he was messed up. He was drunk, and he wanted me to drive his car. I was like cool, but it was a stick shift. He said he would teach me, so he can get home. Well, he tried his best, but all I know is I was messing his gears up left and right, jerking all the way down Burleigh Street. The closer we got to the house the more comfortable I started getting with shifting the gears and mashing the clutch at the same time; I got the hang of it. He kept telling me to get a car that was a stick shift, he said it would save on gas and I would like it.

My brother Elvis was the most fly dude I knew besides my dad, and man I just really wanted to be like him in so many ways. You know how you compare yourself to your bigger brother? That's what I was doing. To me, he had everything that I thought I wanted to have. He was tall, everybody liked him, and he was like the talk of the city as far as I was concerned. Like my dad, if you made Elvis upset he wasn't playing any games. He wasn't doing any talking, he was going to get it on. It was in them, there's nothing he could have done about that. I didn't think Elvis feared anything, until he was going to be a firefighter and during training they sent them out to a real fire in which a man got burned up. That messed him up. He said he couldn't be a firefighter after that. He was saying the smell took him some place where he just couldn't imagine being a firefighter anymore. A lot of times I think he used to come to Westlawn just to get me out of there. He knew that it was bad over there and rough, but he always made sure that we were good.

I ended up getting an Escort GT, black on black, trying to be like my big BROTHER. Man, we used to have so much fun! I was going to different places, clubs, and to the lakefront. Me, him and Murphy, we had a ball. Sometimes I used to sneak off down south and he'd be there. They would just laugh. As we got older life was starting to hit him really good. Elvis's mother passed away and that just was devastating for him. I remember talking to him while he was at the airport in Atlanta and I could hear the hurt in his voice. He needed to talk to somebody very badly, and he called me. All he wanted me to do was just pray. For the first time in my life I found myself being the big brother to him.

REROUTED

It's amazing how God reverses your thinking as you get older. He certainly did that to me and Elvis, I don't think we ever talked about the Bible and God more than we did the next couple of weeks. Today, we both drive trucks and every Wednesday will call each other to see what route we had and how far down the road we are. You see, I always saw Elvis on Tuesdays and Thursdays and Sundays because we had church.

Elvis helped me change my thinking, he would never allow me to think that somebody else is better than me. He would say that man put his pants on just like you do, don't ever think somebody better than you. He had a unique ability to uplift you and for you to believe that you were even better than you were.

THE STREET LIFE

Have you ever been some places and you just didn't fit in? For me that was hustling/street life. My mom was ready to leave the city for good, so she packed up the house and asked me if I was coming to Fordyce with her and my brother Cal, I said no I would be ok making it on my own. I was 20 years old with a son who was about to turn 1 and I had to make some money.

    I decided to make money on the streets hustling. My cousins had put me on the dope game and showed me how to make and keep money in my pocket. I enjoyed going to the Grand Mall in downtown Milwaukee back in the day and buying whatever I wanted. It felt good not looking to see how much it cost, I just got it. However, I didn't like the constant looking over my shoulder, because the block I was on was getting money or just watching out for the police. I was messing around with several women; and that was like

REROUTED

a job lying to all of them, so I could keep up with who I was talking to and controlling when I would see who.

I recall it like it was yesterday going to this spot called "CC" right off 3rd and Keefe Ave. in Milwaukee. I was having a good time. The *"last calls for alcohol,"* was heard over the speakers, so me, my cousins, and some friends began to leave the place. There was this guy sitting on the hood of his car and he said to me, *"I like that "E" you got on your gold chain, you Eric Rainey, right?"* I got suspicious and said what up and then he saw my cousin and was like pop the trunk on these dudes. I didn't know at the time he was with other guys in different cars, they started shooting at us with all types of guns. It had just gotten real to me, I was running for my life and bullets were flying past me. All of this because of jealousy of somebody else making more money than the next man. That was crazy to me, because we all could eat if it wasn't so much hating.

As I look back at this event, I thank God for protecting me from the bullets that were aimed at me. I had already prepared myself to go to the Army, I signed up months before this incident happened. God has a way of making sure that whatever he wants done, gets done. I stayed in Milwaukee another 2 months before I left for the army.

I was stationed in Ft. Carson when I got a call that my cousin Mike had been shot. I started reflecting on how we were always together, Mike made sure that I was good at all times and on all levels. Now he was fighting for his life and I was not there, I was devastated. That could have been me going to turn the alarm off his car and being shot myself, I know this because the alarm used to always go off and I would go and turn it off.

My Lord and My God you saved my cousin's life while taking me away, knowing what was down the road. I couldn't see it back then, but God led me away to a different state far away from what I was used too, he simply rerouted my path and I took that detour. The only reason for me signing up for the Army was my son. I just wanted my son Erik Prescott to have better and to see me doing something that was good. It's funny how having a child can reroute your whole understanding about life. I went from an extreme high of running the streets, to slowing down and looking at the big picture of what life is truly about.

I must admit that the streets were not the ideal place for me, but it taught me some valuable lessons along the way. I couldn't see how hustling would impact my life today, you see you must be disciplined to really be engaged the way you needed to be in the streets. You couldn't really do a lot of hanging out with your homies if you were really trying to get money. You developed a memory of those around you, of what they looked like and sound like, and you didn't tell everybody what your next move was. Today I still use those principles, when I am studying the word of God or even writing a book I can't do a lot of hanging out,

REROUTED

even if it means missing a big party that everyone is at. You have to be on the grind for what matters most in your life. When I greeted at the door of the church, I would remember the faces and names that would normally come through the doors of the church and greeted them accordingly.

The truth is I wasn't really that goon, straight up thug dude ruling the streets. I grew up amongst the vampires who preyed on the night zombies looking for a fix. I simply had a pass, because of the "cred" (street credit) that my cousins had. I'm just stating the fact that we all have some sort of hustle, but it doesn't have to be bad in one's sight. We all can't be big time street pharmacists, some of us were not cut out for that. Maybe your hustle is flipping houses or playing the stock market to see if you could come up quick. Just understand what side of the track you belong and don't try to be what you are not. I used to struggle within my heart because deep down inside I wanted to be like my cousins and to make it happen at any given time out here in the streets. I grew up amongst them and they took care of me, so I know what this is all about. I just didn't like it, I didn't see the importance of fighting someone and beating somebody down over a dollar. I didn't care for that at all. I know it's about the principles and the understanding of the street code. To see women with children walking around with pampers on, coming up to you to buy this or that I didn't like that, but I also knew if I wanted some money I had to give them what they asked for.

ERIC RAINEY

Street life is a dirty game and I found out that wasn't my lane. I think sometimes we make the mistake of really trying to be something we're not and are afraid to admit that is not who we are. I found out that most people respect those individuals who know who they are and where they belong. I just believe it is beneficial to everyone involved, that way they know I don't have to watch over my shoulder for this guy, he isn't really trying to be out here like that. He's just trying to get some money, he not trying to be no Kingpin and that's what it is. I've seen too many guys who live the street life and that wasn't them, they held onto something that didn't even fit. I am so glad I did have the experience though, because now when I witness about Jesus I can go to those same neighborhoods and not be afraid.

My past has helped me to reroute my thinking about the streets, I'm here to serve God's people. I am in no way advocating for one to be a dope man. I am simply stating facts that too many men front about being a dough boy and are scared to keep it real. I knock no man for trying to feed his family, but I know a better way, not only to feed your family but to have peace while doing it.

It seemed to me that trouble just followed me. I was on my way to Whitewater University to visit a lady friend of mine, so I invited my friend Terrance. We called him Boo. When I picked Boo up he decided he didn't want to go, and he wanted to be dropped off

REROUTED

where his girlfriend was. I kept asking him was he sure because they're having a party at Whitewater and it's going to be off the chain. He was like yeah, I'm sure. So, I say cool, I drop him off and I head up to Whitewater not knowing that would be the last time I would see him.

He had got into an altercation with some guys at a bar and he proceeded to beat up 3 guys and one of them wasn't having it. One of the guys went to his house and brought back a shotgun and shot Boo and killed him. I recall calling my mother for some strange reason and when she picked the phone up she was in an uproar. She kept saying, *"where are you, where are you, are you okay?"* I say yes, I'm fine Mom. All of a sudden, she bust out crying and said, *"Please come home Boo got killed and I thought you guys were together."* I told my mom before I left for Whitewater that I was picking up Boo and that's where we were going. I can imagine the stress, pain, and frustration that she had all night wondering where I was. I had no idea all this was going on, and it hurt me bad just to hear her say those words. I think I drove a hundred miles per hour coming back from Whitewater just so I could hold my mother. I remember Boo just getting a Dallas Cowboys Starter jacket. Back then people were robbing folks for those jackets. I found out that they weren't trying to rob him, and he was only protecting himself and his girlfriend. I wasn't in a kind mood. I couldn't even talk to his mother after all this, everybody in Westlawn was devastated and was ready for war.

ERIC RAINEY

I am so glad that God stepped in and took matters into his own hands, the man who shot Boo was arrested and sent to prison. When I think about this tragic situation I recall how I used to blame myself for not convincing my friend to stay in the car and ride with me. I can still picture in my mind me throwing him a lob and he would catch it and dunk on some dude 6"8. I know now that God had rerouted my steps that day, because he never asked me to stay with him instead of going to Whitewater, he simply said E, go have some fun. Don't take your friendship with anyone for granted, you never know when your last conversation with them will be.

CHAPTER SIX

LOVE LOST TO BEGIN LOVE

When I got out of the military I came back to Milwaukee and my life started to change in an unexpected way. I remember getting the call that my grandmother passed away. I just fell to my knees and cried for hours. In my heart I felt no one cared for me like she did. I recall standing on her porch waiting for her to come home from her job. I just started reflecting on what she meant to me and what she left behind. I loaded up my car, picked up my son up and headed to Arkansas to lay my grandma to rest.

    I noticed a white bird while I was driving on I-57 near Champaign, IL, this bird seemed like it was following me. Everything I stopped for, gas or to use the restroom, that white bird was right there. Once we made it to Little Rock, Arkansas the bird disappeared.

ERIC RAINEY

I felt a connection with that beautiful white bird, the bird was guiding me looking down on me, it was amazing. I truly believed my grandmother's spirit was in that bird. My heart would beat faster the further I drove, and the bird was still around. I could feel my grandmother, I could even smell her fragrance. I tell you, I could see her face with the gold tooth she had. I could see it right in front of my face.

Cancer was the culprit that took my grandmother's life. Two months before she passed I went to visit her in the hospital, I was devastated to see her in that state. I remember she wanted a swab of water and she told me to lean in so she could tell me something. What she told me was the beginning of the shift of my life, I call it the day God was rerouting my life. In a very faint voice she said, *"Eric, you are a special one."* I say ok grandma I know. I was trying to get her not to talk because she was very weak. She sat up a little in the bed and said it again, *"You are a special one."* I paused this time and I looked directly at her eyes and I knew she was serious. It was a take heed to what I'm saying to you because I won't be here much longer, moment. That's why that white bird was so significant, because I started to think about our conversation, which was our last conversation.

I was told to say some words about my grandmother, mind you I did not grow up in church and really did not know where I was supposed to be. They called me up to speak and I walked past the microphone that was set up for me to speak and I walked straight into the pulpit. Yes I did. I could see the facial expressions, like what are you doing. I put my hands on the pulpit and thought I felt a shock that went through my hands and my entire body. I proceeded to take out my written words, but I heard a voice that said speak from your heart. I could not even remember what I said I just know it was an outer body experience, something I never felt before.

As I looked back on that day, the pastor of that church came to me and asked me a question he said, *"Hey son is you a preacher?"* My respond was, *"No sir I am a rapper."* He looked at me in my eyes and said, *"You were taking your rightful place up there when you were speaking this time."* I said ok thanks and walked away from him hoping he didn't follow me. I was trying to duck off to myself, so I could be alone. My aunt Joyce's husband Mack came over to talk to me. Mack asked me was I a preacher. I said, *"No Mack I am not a preacher, nor will I ever be."* Now I am beginning to wonder why everybody is saying the same thing to me. I heard what they all said about who they thought I may be, but I was not convinced at all, not me. I used to tell my aunts Jean and Fay, *"Y'all go to church all the time just giving the preacher your money and you don't know that man like that."* I couldn't see myself being in church and preaching the Word of God, which I knew nothing about.

God will always tell or warn you of what's down the

road. Either you will believe it or he will surely make a believer out of you. Who would have ever thought that the young man who wouldn't step foot in a church as a teenager would become a preacher? My grandmother knew this all along, she just didn't tell me what it was before she took flight. I guess this explains why she protected me so much, she even threatened my grandfather if he would put one hand on me she was going hit him in the head with a coke bottle. I often wonder what God said to her about me. I can only imagine what was said. Sometimes I'm just chilling at home and I can hear her say my name, and I look as if she is standing there with that one gold tooth shining like it had diamonds. I know my grandmother is smiling right now, saying Erica, that's how she pronounced my name. She had no idea the seed she planted when she let me know I was a special one. Although her voice was faint, it got the job done.

The one person who I felt loved me the most, has handed me over to the one who says he would never leave me nor forsake me. So now when I come in contact with an elderly person who wants to talk to me I sit down and listen intentionally. I've learned seasoned people want to pass down knowledge and often times we pushed them away or cut them off. I just don't want to miss the point like I did some years ago when my grandmother was trying to tell me who I was. One day I too will become old and I'm hoping that I will be able to pass down knowledge and information that I know. I asked God to forgive me for not obeying what

REROUTED

was said to me. I didn't know any better, but I should have asked someone what she was trying to say to me. Nevertheless, I finally took the detour, and I get it. My life was rerouted from the beginning of time.

THE ENCOUNTERS WITH GOD

Have you ever been just strolling through life when something just completely knocks you off your feet?

Well one day in December of 1998 I had an encounter with God that changed my life forever. I was driving home from work and I decided to stop at KFC to get me some food to take home. After I got my food I walked back to my car and a man stopped me and asked me for some money. I tell this man I don't got nothing for him and he needs to move around. When I pulled up to my house I began to get out the car and a car drove fast by me, so I quickly closed my car door and was thinking what's up with that person. I began to laugh, and I heard a voice say, *"Go and give that man your coat and money."* I was scared because I thought this person was in my car in the back seat, so I eased

REROUTED

my head around to see who was back there. There wasn't anybody in the back seat. Then that same voice said to me, *"Go and give that man your coat and money."* I started my car and said, *"Lord is this you? That man is gone by now, tell me where he is now."* The Lord told me to turn right at the stop sign and then another right at next stop sign and another right. I did exactly as I was instructed, and that same man was standing in the middle of an alley behind the police station. I proceeded to get out of my car, took my coat off and I gave to him along with the money I had in my pocket. Something strange happened after I gave him everything I was supposed to. He didn't say thank you. He simply said, *"Who sent you?"* I told him the Lord sent me sir, take care.

I didn't know the scriptures back then, but in Acts 9: 3-4 there was a man named Saul who was on the road to Damascus and suddenly there shined round about him a light from heaven; and he fell to the earth, and heard a voice saying unto him Saul, Saul why persecutes thou me? I can relate to this because that is exactly how I felt when I heard His voice, I even said is this you Lord not knowing what He sounds like, I just knew it was Him.

I felt good for some reason. It was cold outside, snowing and now I have no coat. I called my mother to let her know what I had experienced, let's just say she wasn't happy with me. I think she thought I lost my mind. So, I went from being happy and feeling good, to thinking, *"what did I just do?"* Later that evening a lady I knew stopped by, she said she wanted to give me something. This lady had brought me a brand-new leather coat, she was like I thought it would look good on you, so I got it. I knew at that moment it was God who did that. It almost felt like I was dreaming, like really, this is happening to me!

A month later I had another encounter with the Lord, but this time he didn't speak. I went to a liquor store after work and bought a six pack and a half-pint of whiskey. I remember getting home and I opened a beer, but when I started drinking it tasted horrible, like it was stale. I asked my brother D was his beer stale, he was like no bro its good and cold. I picked up the bottle of whiskey, slapped the bottom of the bottle a couple of times and popped the top and took me a sip. I couldn't believe it, it was horrible too. I went back to the liquor store and bought another six pack of beer and another half-pint of whiskey. Same nasty taste, God had taken the taste of alcohol right from me just like that.

I was wondering what was going on with me and why was I am feeling like that. I remembered my sister Kim Edwards telling me one day that Willie Clyde was once an alcoholic and they got pulled over one time and they put them both in jail. God didn't want that to be passed down to me, so He just took matters into His own hands and broke that generational curse.

I'm telling you God is in control whether you like or

REROUTED

not, he can do whatever he wants, when he wants. Don't be uneasy when he starts to work out his plans for you. I believe we all have or will have an encounter with God on some level. It doesn't matter where you are, you could be at the barbershop, the grocery store, or just walking through your city. I promise you will hear somebody talking about the Lord as if you were meant to hear it, and you were. Our encounters will differ from the next person, but indeed one can almost be certain that encounter will arrive. Even in the Bible some encounters were so unbelievable they had to be documented. When Moses led God's people to the Red Sea he didn't expect what was about to happen, God told Moses to stretch out his staff and part the Red Sea. Can you imagine the facial expressions on all those people's faces when the sea opened up and they began to walk on dry land through the Red Sea? What an encounter they experienced at that very moment. Expect the unexpected when your encounter comes.

    I had a gentleman get on the Greyhound bus with me as I was riding the bus to Chicago to take a schedule to Memphis. This particular gentleman sat next to me and said some things that startled me because he had an impediment in his speech, but it seemed like his impediment went away and he turned to me and said, *"If You Don't Preach you're going to lose your legs."* You talking about an encounter? I immediately called my wife and talked to her grandfather (Apostle Elbridge Lock) and he said he wanted to call me right back. He prayed about it and he told me yes, that is true. I could not believe it, a man who really couldn't talk turned and looked at me and talked like he was an English professor. Are you kidding me? What an encounter with God. These days I never brush people off when they tell me they had an encounter with God, or they had a situation that they couldn't believe and was scared to say I think it was God. I just smile because I know how they feel. I try to encourage everyone who has an encounter of some sort to talk with their spiritual leaders and tell them exactly what's going on, so they can help along the way with their experience. What a mighty God we serve that He will allow us to have encounters with Him and not consuming us in our sins. Oh, let us magnify His name together!

MARRIED TO THAT LIFE

May 17, 2003, I married the love of my life Kimberly Owens. God had given me a glimpse of this amazing woman of God when I was 8 years old. We lived in the same projects as kids, Parklawn, and went to Sunday school together, go figure. First off, I didn't learn anything in Sunday school back then, I was sleep and so was my little brother De. Kim seemed so little back then, I couldn't even imagine being married to her. We got disconnected when my family moved back to Arkansas, but when we moved back to Milwaukee De would always tell me he saw her and her sister Woochie. I never paid too much attention to what he was saying, I was living the dream, at least that's what I thought. However, as time went by I ended up seeing her at a church called Unity Gospel House of Prayer. I was about to get married to someone else at that time, but that never happened. I saw Kim in a dream, and in this dream, she was my wife.

Now, I have heard His voice before and I knew it was the Lord, but this here was Kim from Parklawn. So, I told my cousin Melissa and she was so happy. Eventually I told Kim at church who she was, and will she marry me, and she said yes. It was told to her by Kaysha, Kim's, friend that she is about to marry a man whose name starts with an E. Can you believe that? Her best friend had a dream like that and there I was. Kim's granddad even had a dream and asked her had she been talking to the Lord about a husband. She says she hadn't, and her grandad told her he is coming. Really! Now here comes the kicker. Her granddad was the pastor of the church, Apostle Elbridge Lock. I sat down with him and her grandma Prophetess Naomi Lock, they gave us their blessing and we got married. We have 8 children, 2 of them are grown and married, Erik, and Ciera. The rest of our children, Marquis, Grace, Caleb, Luke, Gabby, and Naomi are at home with us.

Our marriage has had its share of problems, from me not wanting to commit all the way to Lord and me being gone most of the time driving Greyhound around the country. I'm sure my wife didn't see that coming being married, I'm certain she felt alone. She was around her grandparents every day, she knew what marriage should look like and be like. I didn't have that example, as far as being God-fearing husband. I was lying, moody, and I felt she was trying to force me into a lifestyle I thought I wasn't ready for. One day she just

REROUTED

got fed up, we started arguing and we got into a fight. The police came and took me to jail.

The lowest part of my life it seemed, but the strangest thing happened, I got released the next day which was a Sunday. In Milwaukee if you are picked up by the police on Saturday usually you are there until Monday. I ended up staying at my brother's house for some days, but I was miserable, and I had to ask for forgiveness. I went to church that Tuesday and stood before the congregation and asked them all to forgive me for my wrong. I couldn't understand why I had to do it that way, but that's the way I was led.

Many men came up to me and said I helped them, some of them had similar issues. I knew God was working even when I was broken. I had many sleepless nights wondering and praying, hoping that God would step in my situation and fix what was wrong.

We eventually got back together, but this time on one accord. My wife became pregnant with our youngest child Naomi and the doctor told her she needed to be on bed rest. Kim said she felt fine and nothing was wrong with her, but God had a plan and it was going to be executed. She ended up in the hospital for 3 months, that meant I had to come off my job driving for Greyhound. Naomi came into this world 2 months premature, April 15, 2013. She was so small, I asked the nurse was my daughter going to survive; she couldn't even look at me and answer me.

I immediately called my pastor, Pastor Marlon

Lock, who just happened to be my brother-in-law and told him to get to the hospital right away. He came and put a prayer cloth on her and we were surprised because the hospital usually doesn't allow anyone to put anything on a child that's in the intensive care unit. I couldn't even pick her up, we had to wear special gloves and gowns just to put the prayer cloth on. Marlon could tell I was bothered, so he quickly rerouted my thinking and told me about another member's child who could fit in his hand. He began to explain to me if God can help that family, surely, he will help our family.

God moved in a mighty way, the doctors thought Naomi would stay in the hospital for months, she got out the hospital three weeks after she was born. God changed what man said to show me he is in charge, and there is none beside him. The whole entire pregnancy I thought was about my wife and baby Naomi, I was so wrong. I found out it was mostly about me. God knew I wasn't coming off my job on my own, so he arranged the proper circumstances to occur to get what he wanted accomplished. I was at church every time the doors opened, doing whatever needed to be done. God certainly changed my narrative and I was following his plan.

I really wanted to show you how God rerouted my marriage, and if you ever get low in your marriage talk to the true counselor, JESUS. You will never have a better counselor, confidant, or friend than Jesus. Once you are in right standing with God he will do wonders

REROUTED

for you, he will move mountains that look impossible to move. God can use any situation, so he can get the glory out of it, he takes pleasure in doing things that man doesn't think is going to happen.

CHURCH

I used to think church people were way too anti-social, and if you weren't with them you were against them. I didn't understand it at first, not wanting to be around certain people because they drink, or smoke weed or anything of that nature. I didn't understand, I thought church people were to help people and help save people, not run away from them. I didn't know they were just being to themselves so they wouldn't fall back into the trap that they used to be in; whether it be drinking or smoking or doing drugs or whatever the case may be, I just didn't know it at the time.

My aunts Jean, Fay, and Betty used to always talk about how good service was at church. I couldn't believe that they would be at church Sunday morning, Sunday night, Tuesday night, and Thursday night. It was like they lived there. I thought something was wrong with them, but they had a peace about them that was

REROUTED

like a graceful walk on a summer day. I started watching them like an FBI agent watching a serial killer. One Sunday night I was at Aunt Jean house and they all walked in from Sunday night service on fire. Me being curious, I ask what happened and that's when the name Pastor Elbridge Lock came out of their mouths. I began to be intrigued about this man. I decided to attend the service and I was blown away by his knowledge and understanding of the word.

I'd seen some preachers before and they all look like the pastor in Coming to America, so seeing this man was like a breath of fresh air. I didn't grow up in church, but I knew this man was different. He said for most of his life he couldn't read but now he can read the Bible because of the Holy Ghost. I believed what he said and from that day I started my journey on this Christian walk.

The beginning of this journey was horrible. I married into a family full of preachers, talk about pressure. I went from never wanted to preach, to being called to preach; not knowing anything about the Bible and people want me to preach. I needed help bad. I was trying to cover up, I didn't know and was too prideful to ask for help. I kept comparing myself to my in-laws, their lives looked like everyone had it all together spiritually and naturally. I felt like I didn't fit in and I couldn't identify the signs that were set before me, because I ignored them all.

My wife's Granddad who happened to be the

pastor would always say, *"Son obey God, He will bless you real good,"* or *"Son keep your faith in God,"* or how about, *"Son are you paying your tithes and offering."* The whole time I would be listening and thinking like what is he talking about. I was so busy trying to please the man himself but never pleasing God. I couldn't understand how a man who could not read, could understand God's word like he was there in the beginning. However, I could read, and the Bible was like a foreign language. I was in the boat going nowhere, just drifting in the middle of the ocean. If I only knew what I know now, I would have prayed and asked the Lord to get in my boat.

I was trying really hard to figure church out. Imagine not knowing any church songs, no church hymns, none of that; and when everybody starts singing you trying to keep up and keep the pace, but you can't. In the back of my mind I wish I knew these songs. I wish in my childhood that I had the opportunity to go to church with my family, and everybody sat and sang songs and hymns and clapped. I wish we talked about Jesus and worshipped and praised Him, but that just wasn't my reality and I suffered during that time. Finally, I started to get a little glimpse of what church was about I started feeling good about myself and who I was.

The pastor asked me to read the scriptures while he preached. I started to learn more and more. My confidence grew, but then suddenly, out of nowhere my mind went carnal and I decided I wanted to leave and drive a truck and I didn't want to be in church. I remember vividly the pastor talking about not leaving the church and just being still and holding on to God otherwise you're going to have a shipwreck. Eventually I decided to drive a truck, then I didn't like it and came right back and tried to get in where I fit in at church. I was only gone for about 2 or 3 weeks, but it seemed like I was gone for a year and I set myself back just in a little amount of time because I was still debating Christ and didn't know anything.

My wife's Granddad and I didn't see eye-to-eye for a little while and I think that hurt me as well, because once again I was trying to please man and not God. I just didn't understand it at that time but as time went on we reconciled, and I started to understand what this walk was all about, but he was getting ill in his body and eventually passed away April 8, 2009. The man who I thought could help me to understand the words of the Bible like he did, was gone and now his grandson, Pastor Marlon Lock, was taking over.

I was thinking, man he younger than me how is he going to teach me the Word of God, but I'll tell you what, it turned out to be a blessing in disguise. Although Pastor Marlon Lock was young, he was gritty, and he knew what he was talking about because he was called at the age of five and his teaching and preaching was phenomenal. He took me in under his wing and showed me what it was all about, he even encouraged me to start sitting on the front row so I can feel and see how a preacher moves and talks, his mannerisms. I loved every moment of it. Eventually he would put me in a Minister's class to really get the knowledge and understanding of how a minister should be and what things ministers are supposed to do. I was growing really fast and my confidence was building really high. One would think that would be a good thing. It was for a moment, but then it turned out to be bad. I was thinking that I was in control. I was not in control, it was always God. It had nothing to do with me and it had all to do with the Lord, but that's just part of growing up in Christ. Marlon would always say, *"Hey bro don't take your gift for granted always give it back to the Lord and understand it's not you."* I used to hear him say it but at that time I really didn't understand. He knew what he was talking about because he experienced it as well. I found out that the gift God gives you is for you to serve others and to help others, not to bring yourself glory. I didn't understand it at that point but now I do. I couldn't see it, but now I can. The reason I couldn't see it was because I was still carnal minded, but God rerouted my mindset to understand the Heavenly things and how it works. It's about you, it's about others and loving others and serving others. I began to serve more at the church; greeting, outreach team, parking lot team, whatever was asked. I just wanted to be able to serve and serve well. I wanted God to be pleased with me, so my mission became to be the best servant I could be. I recall getting a call from my pastor, Pastor Marlon Lock,

REROUTED

to preach my first message. I was so nervous and so scared. Oh my goodness! However, when you're called, this what you're called to do. As nervous as I was I went to sleep like it wasn't nothing. My wife was saying, *"How could you sleep at a time like this, aren't you nervous?"* I said, *"Yeah I am, but I found out when I'm real nervous I sleep better."* I got up to preach and I was shaking, my legs were shaking my arms were shaking my hands were shaking, Lord help! Eventually my nerves calmed down and I finished my first message. I was so happy! I was just ready to go home get away from everybody and go to sleep. I didn't know preaching takes so much out of you, especially when you give your all it's almost like playing a basketball game. I was tired and drained.

Some days I wish I could go back and see the old pastor in Fordyce and tell him he was right, and I was so wrong, and ask him to forgive me because he knew something I didn't know. I will always be grateful to Pastor Marlon Lock for taking me under his wing and showing me what a minister or preacher should be like. He also took ten of us to TD Jakes's *"Pastors and Leadership Conference"* in Florida some years ago. It was phenomenal, and we learned so much that we implemented some of those things at our church. Now I have gone annually to the TD Jakes pastoral leadership conference and I must say every time that I have gone I have learned.

I am so ever grateful to my Pastor and his wife, Lady Kim Lock, for having a vision to see beyond and allowing us to go to learn and get better not only as ministers and preachers but as human beings and business people as well. I also found out that the church is not the building the church is you, the church is in the inside of you. What God has put into you is for you to pour it into someone else and lead and guide them and help them on their journey. Just as Apostle Elbridge Lock, Prophetess Naomi Lock, Pastor Marlon Lock, and First Lady Kim lock have shared and helped others grow to become great men and women of God. I must give my wife credit as well because she was the one to deal with me all the time, yet she encouraged me to keep reading to and keep studying. She always said that God was going to plant his Word inside of me if I continued to do those things, and she was right. Church is just not on Sundays behind the pulpit, church is in your community, church is at your work, church is at the park, church is when you lay down, church is when you get up, church is everywhere with you because it's in you. I thank God for allowing me to finally understand what church is about. To change a life into a better life and life full of God's promises - His joy, His peace, His kindness – you must reroute your life and take that detour before you destroy your life.

I'm blessed to have so many spiritual influences in my life, some near and dear to my heart and some I don't know personally. I try to take a little bit from each of them as I grow into my own.

Apostle Elbridge Lock showed me what a leader

REROUTED

was all about. He also showed me what God can do to any human being who has desire to be great, and what God called him to do. His faith in God was impeccable. He leaned and depended on Him only. I'm so glad that God allowed me to start my journey in ministry with the Apostle.

Pastor Marlon Lock brings a lot of energy and enthusiasm while he preaches and is very passionate about the ability that God gave to him. His constant drive to get better as a pastor and businessman is infectious.

G.E. Patterson, whom I never met, but I watched a whole lot of his sermons on the Word Network and on YouTube, and I love the way he brings the Word and is passionate about our Lord and Savior Jesus Christ. His reflection about his father's grandfather and how they ministered the Word as well, let me know that the family tradition was being carried on and he was determined to carry out what the Lord has set before him.

Bishop TD Jakes also is a big influence on me in the way that he delivers his word and a charismatic way that engages me like no other. I have never met the Bishop, but I have been to three of his pastors' and leaders' conferences and I also have been to The Potter's House.

I used to get a natural high when listening to Tupac, Scarface, and Jay-Z, now I get that high from listening to these great men of God. God has truly rerouted my tune, I went from nodding my head to my favorite rappers, to clapping and praising God to my favorite preachers. Lord I Thank you.

TRAGEDY TO HOPE

Have you ever got that phone call in the middle of the night that you knew no one calls you at that time but something was wrong? I did. March 13, 2018 I was getting ready to get back in the bed and I got a phone call from my brother Kevin about 4a.m. He asked me if I heard or did anybody call me about my cousin Nisha dying. I told him no one called me how about that and I asked him who told him that and he said my cousin Tank. I called Tank immediately and he said, *"Cuz, Nisha is dead. She got shot in a drive-by shooting in Little Rock, Arkansas."* My heart just dropped. Nisha was more like a niece to me than my cousin. I couldn't believe that someone had killed her.

My whole family was grieving, Nisha was so kind to all of us, to everyone that encountered her. There was nothing that she wouldn't do for you. If you needed a place to stay she would open her home for you to stay. If you needed some money and she had it she would give it to you. She was just that type of person and we all knew it and we all took this one very hard. Her mother, my aunt Jean, who is strong in the faith was hurting so bad. I called her, and she was more concerned about me and my brothers than she was about her own self.

Nisha had two children, Shariya and Elias, who were now left without a mother. Nisha's brothers Antrell and Bob were devastated as well. What do you tell them at a time like this when everyone is feeling angry, even my own self? I began to talk to the Lord and ask him to help me to cope with this tragic loss for not only myself, but my aunt, her children and grandchildren.

Not even three days later, tragedy struck once more. My cousin Murphy Jamerson III, who was a healthy, devoted man to God, collapsed in the basement at his home. As was leaving work I received a call that Murphy has no pulse. My wife and I rushed over there believing everything was going to be okay. When we arrived Murphy's dad, sisters, brother, and mother were down in the basement with the paramedics as they tried to revive him. Murphy's wife Lana was sitting on the couch with First Lady Kim Lock. She was devastated, she was the one who found Murphy in the basement after the school had called and said that he didn't pick up his daughter from school.

REROUTED

After about 45 minutes, the paramedics and the fire department said they couldn't do anything else and my cousin Murphy had passed away. I couldn't believe it, I had just talked to Murphy at church and was asking him was he going down south to the family reunions and he looked at me and said, *"Cuz you know what, I don't know."* That was the last time I heard his voice. I just remember everybody started crying. To see his dad, my brother Murphy, to see him in so much pain and hurt was devastating. To see his brother Quentiel and his sisters Cortina, Maquetia and Breasia's faces with so much grief and pain, I just couldn't bear it anymore. To watch his wife looking in disbelief on the back porch crying, and my wife and I hollered.

My entire family was devastated. Back to back devastation took a toll on all of us. We were planning on going to Arkansas to bury my cousin Nisha, now who would plan the burial of Murphy in Milwaukee. Murphy and his wife Lana have five children, Jasmine, Raina, Muriah, Murphy Jamerson, IV, and Modesty. I couldn't understand what was going on with my family. Where do we go from here? When I'm at church I look up in a choir stand on the righthand side by the stairs to see if Murphy is there. It's just a natural reaction because he always stood there as the pastor's armor bearer, right hand man. Murphy was the chairman of the deacon board and all those guys looked up to him. Murphy was well-loved and would do anything for anyone. My wife called him an angel, because when I was driving Greyhound he made sure my family was okay.

ERIC RAINEY

The family went to Fordyce, Arkansas to bury Nisha Rainey on March 22, 2018 and traveled back to Milwaukee to bury Murphy Lee Jameson the Third on March 26, 2018. As a family we have become closer and vowed to make sure that we attend our family events. Life itself is so precious we don't know how much time we have, so we must take full advantage of the time that we do spend here.

The untimely deaths of my cousins took a deep toll on me. It is one thing to anticipate death for someone who was already ill, but this I wasn't prepared for this at all and it taught me a valuable lesson. I have once again rerouted my understanding about life and death. Sad as it may sound, we were all born but have a date to leave here. Death is something we usually don't plan for, especially in the black community. I know we all must leave here, but I never thought of it like I do now after the death of my cousins.

I know the saying is when you die as a Christian we should all celebrate and rejoice, but the truth of the matter is you also do some mourning and your heart is very heavy. The Bible says in Psalms 150:6, *"Let everything that hath breath praise the Lord. Praise ye the Lord."* (KJV) It never said what kind of condition your breath has to be in, as long as you have breath praise Him. I saw my cousin Cortina Cotton do just that, when Murphy passed she raised her hands and praised the Lord.

Although these tragedies are devastating we have

REROUTED

hope and will continue on and become stronger in our walk with the Lord knowing that He would never leave us or forsake us. Our family reunions will no doubt be better and bigger because of their legacies and because of the commitment not only to the Lord but to our family as well. We will all see each other once again on that great day when we all be caught up.

My pastor always says during the funeral, when it is your time, no one can answer when it is your time to leave here. Therefore, it's critical that we make sure we do things God is pleased with. I'm so glad God uses the number two pencil that has an eraser, because He will use that eraser to erase all the things you did wrong when He has forgiven you of your sins. That's the hope we all should strive for, knowing that this is not our home we are just passing by. I couldn't see what God was trying to tell me when I was writing about this particular chapter, but He wants you to know that you can reroute your legacy by doing things His way. I encourage you to use your glory on Glory. Just like that woman who came to Jesus with the alabaster box and wiped his feet with the ointment, her tears, and her hair which is her glory. She used the very thing that God gave to her as her glory on Jesus who is Glory. She was never the same after that, you also have something to offer, take the detour that has been set right before you and reroute your destination which should be heaven.

CONCLUSION

I hope this book has opened your eyes to take the detour of life and be rerouted. As you reflect on your life and think about where God has brought you from, think about all those moments and times he was right there, and you didn't know it at the time; like from the farm in the deep south to the bright city lights of any major city. Somewhere in your journey God has rerouted you in your life. Maybe you grew up in a single parent home without a father figure, but you made it. If God can take a boy with the odds stacked against him throughout his life and reroute his whole understanding of what life is really about, he can or already has changed your path. Proverbs 14:12 says, *"There is a way which seems right unto a man, but the end thereof are the ways of death."* That is what happens when we don't give it all to the one who is right, God. Who would have ever thought that the very person who thought church was over rated and certainly didn't think anyone should go more than 1 day a week, would become a minister. Remember when you said you would never do this or that? What happened, you ended up doing those things. When you start having those outer body experiences with God or encounters, it's the start of rerouting you from being carnal minded to spiritually minded.

Don't discount your small beginnings it's all a set

up for your future. Romans 8:28 says, *"And we know that all things work together for good to them that love God, to them who are the called according to his purpose."* I am saying although you may have had a rough beginning, it is going to work out for you if you hang in there and trust God. You couldn't see it then but glory to God he will truly reroute your life if you take his detour.

I would like to take this moment to thank everyone who has impacted my life in a manner that has led me to this point of my life, thank you so much.

ACKNOWLEDGEMENTS

Thank you to Author Kimberly Lock and KRL publishing for thinking of me when I couldn't see what I had inside of me. This process has enlightened my eyes to the possibilities which await me in the future. Your efforts to make sure I had whatever I needed to succeed will not be in vain. Thank you to Pastor Marlon Lock for the prayer that gifted my hands, mind, and tongue. Thank you for pushing me to write and to take Thursdays off from service to do class work.

Thank you to my wife Kim for believing in me and putting up with me during this process. From the moment I told you what I was instructed to do about writing this book, you pushed me every day to get this done, even taking the kids out just so I can be in peace to write and think clear, I love you. To my children Erik, Ciera, Marquis, Grace, Caleb, Luke, Gabby, and Naomi, thank so much for putting up with daddy while writing this book. I can still hear your mom say calm down your dad is writing. I love y'all.

Thank you to my mother for all your support and sacrifices through the years. You are an example of what rerouted is all about. To my dad and his wife, thanks for never turning your back on me and raising me. To my siblings, Damian, Kevin, Elvis, Murphy, Linda, and Kim. Love y'all.

Thank you to my grandparents Dan and Velma Rainey,

REROUTED

I just want to say that I love y'all and miss y'all so much. Thank you to all my aunts, uncles, and the entire Rainey, Cranford, Mitchell, Edwards, and Taylor families.

To Eagles International thank you for having the Authors course.

Thank you Jacquise Hale for the amazing artwork for the book cover.

Thank You Apostle Elbridge and Prophetess Naomi Lock for your love and showing me what God will do if you obey him. Most important, I want to thank God for all that he has done. All honor and glory goes to Him.

REFERENCES

1. Maxwell, John C (2014) The 15 Invaluable Laws of Growth. Live Them and Reach Your Potential. New York, NY. Center Street Hachette Book Group
2. The Holy Bible (1972) A Readers Guide to the Holy Bible King James Version Nashville, TN Thomas Nelson Publishers

ABOUT THE AUTHOR

Eric Rainey is a Husband, Dad, Minister, Author, Mentor, and Freelance Writer. Through his trials and tribulations, Eric has an unique ability to bring to life his past struggles, and help men who have lived in adverse conditions escape their past and birth their future. His commitment to be who GOD called him to be has set a fire in his soul to see men of any color, or race set free and delivered from sin.

www.ingramcontent.com/pod-product-compliance
Lightning Source LLC
Chambersburg PA
CBHW052204110526
44591CB00012B/2078